What Goes Up

Must Come Down

by Daniel Shepard

STECK-VAUGHN
Harcourt Supplemental Publishers

www.steck-vaughn.com

What goes up...

must come **down!**

This happens because of a special force.
This force is called gravity.
Gravity pulls all things toward the Earth.

Gravity is always at work.
It is what keeps us on the ground.
Without gravity, we would float away.

Sometimes we can feel gravity.
Gravity makes it hard to climb up a ladder.

But gravity helps to pull us back down.

We feel gravity when we climb a mountain.
Gravity makes it hard to climb up.

But gravity helps to pull us back down.

What else does gravity do?
It makes things fall to the ground.

It makes raindrops fall, too.
Without gravity, there would be no rain.
It would never come down.

There is very little gravity in space.
People in space float high above the Earth.

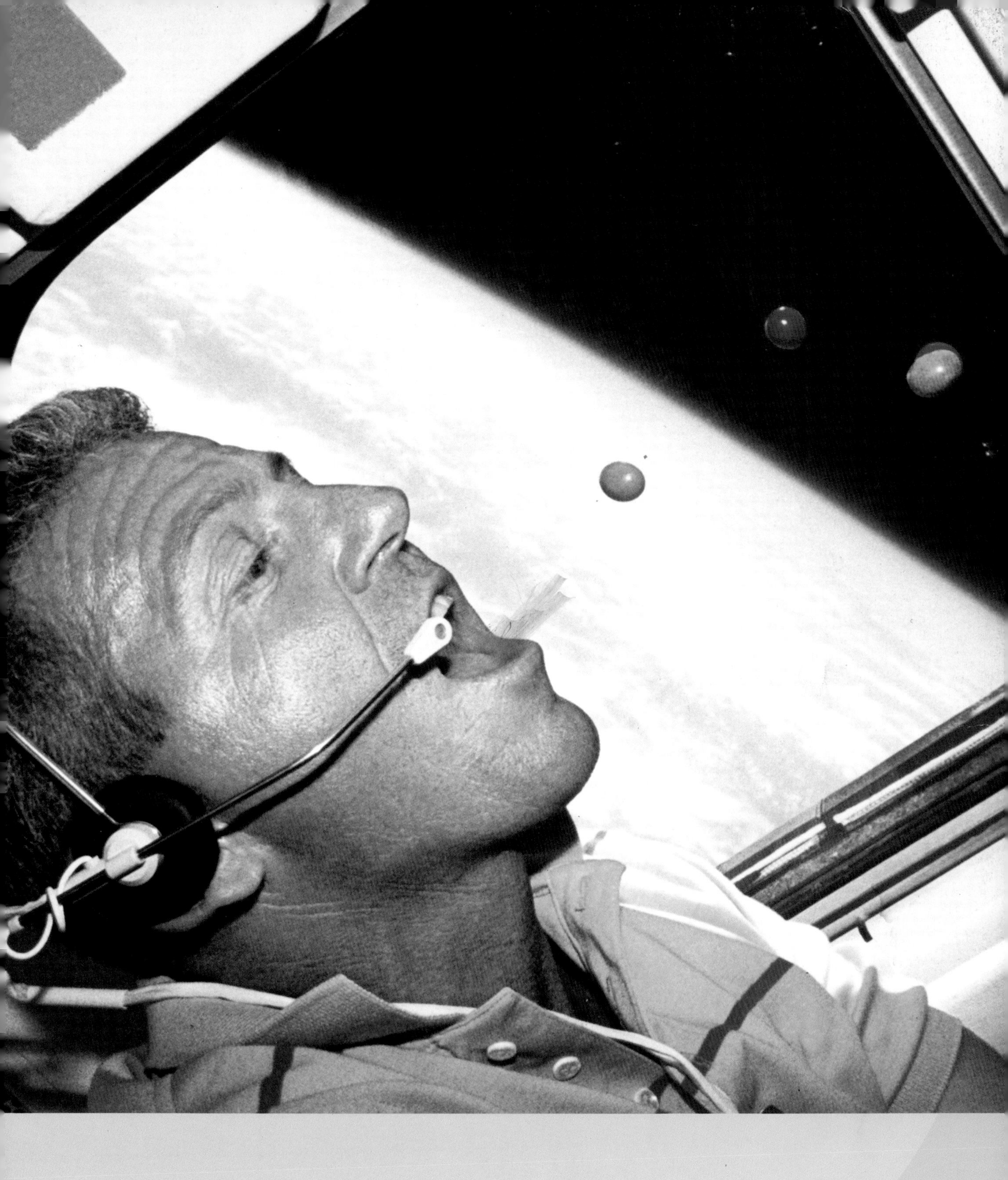

Eating food in space can be tricky.
Without gravity, food can just float away!

We cannot change gravity.
It will always be here, pulling all things toward the Earth.

And that is why what goes up, up, up…

must come down!